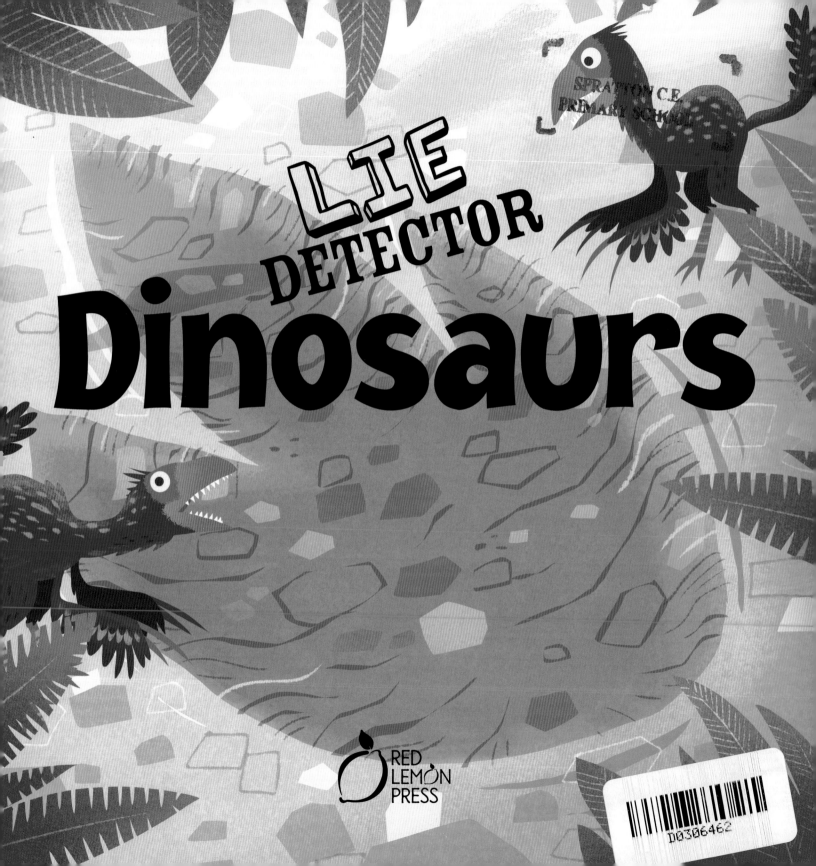

LIE DETECTOR
Dinosaurs

RED LEMON PRESS

RED LEMON PRESS

First published in Great Britain by
Red Lemon Press
Kings Road Publishing
The Plaza
535 King's Road
London SW10 0SZ

All photographs Shutterstock

www.redlemonpress.com
www.bonnierpublishing.com

ISBN: 978-1-7-8342-028-5

Printed in China

10 9 8 7 6 5 4 3 2

LIE DETECTOR
Dinosaurs

WRITTEN BY
Kelly Milner Halls

ILLUSTRATED BY
Lee Cosgrove

Can you reveal the secrets written in stone, and prove you are the master of all things **dinosaur?**

Dinosaurs lived on Earth for more than 160 million years. Then they vanished. No one has ever seen a dinosaur, so how do we know they ever lived? The answer is simple. Dinosaurs left thousands of clues we call fossils. These rocky bits of bone are puzzle pieces that tell amazing stories.

Do you know the facts about fossils – the dish on dinosaurs? Dig into these fun fact-or-fib questions to test your prehistoric knowledge.

Fewer than **10** types of dinosaur have been discovered.

FACT or FIB?

FIB!

More than 700 different kinds of dinosaur have been unearthed, and more are being found every day. Scientists think that many more are waiting to be discovered.

Super sleuth

Kids have found brand new dinosaur species, including Zuniceratops. It was discovered in the USA by 8-year-old Christopher Wolfe.

FACT or FIB?

All dinosaurs were the size of giants.

FIB!

Dinosaurs could be as small as a sparrow, such as Epidendrosaurus, or as long as three school buses lined up end-to-end, like Supersaurus.

ALL GROWN UP?

Many dino discoveries that were thought to be little adults turned out to be regular-sized babies. But some small dinosaurs were just small dinosaurs.

Brachiosaurus and Triceratops were fierce enemies.

FACT or FIB?

FIB!

Dinosaurs ruled the Earth during three different stretches of time called 'periods' – the Triassic Period, the Jurassic Period and the Cretaceous Period. Brachiosaurus lived in the Jurassic and Triceratops lived in the Cretaceous, so they never met.

THE JURASSIC
PERIOD

THE CRETACEOUS
PERIOD

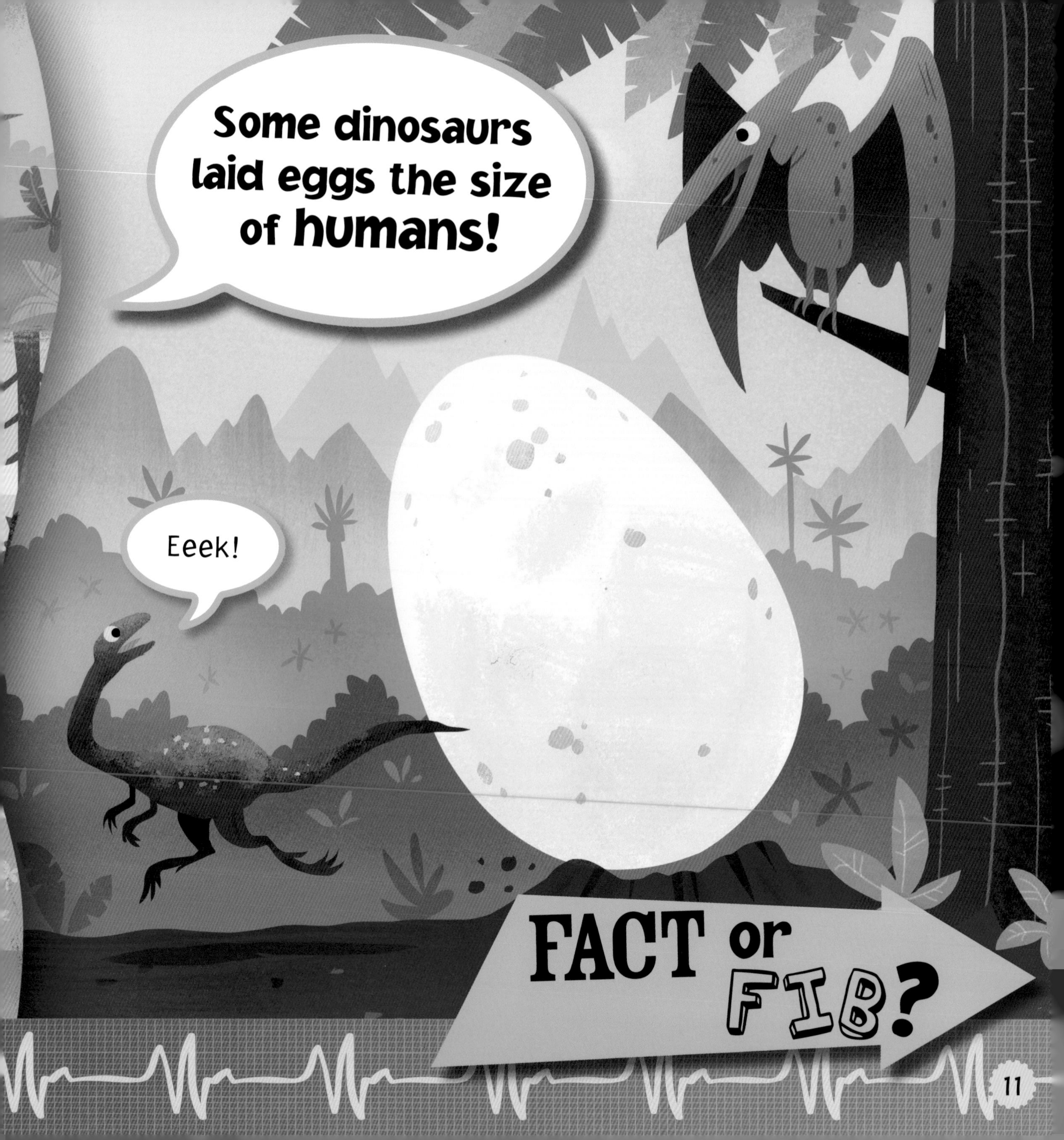
Some dinosaurs laid eggs the size of humans!
Eeek!
FACT or FIB?

FIB!

Dinosaur eggs came in many shapes and sizes – from the size of a golf ball to the size of a baguette. But they were not giant. So far, no dinosaur egg as big as a human has been discovered.

Mmm! Crunchy!
Some plant-eating dinosaurs loved to gobble up rocks too.
FACT or FIB?

FACT!

Long-necked dinosaurs called sauropods swallowed stones on purpose. Those rocks helped to grind up the food inside their stomachs, even after they had finished chewing it with their teeth. Chickens do the same thing today.

All dinosaurs had **scaly** skin.

FACT or FIB?

FIB!

One of the smallest dinosaurs, Pegomastax from Africa, had porcupine-like quills. Many other dinosaurs had soft, downy feathers too – especially when they first hatched.

Insects have existed since the time of the dinosaurs.

FACT or FIB?

Buzz off!

FACT!

Many of the insects that you see today also lived with your favourite dinosaurs, including ants, bees, wasps, spiders, gnats and mosquitoes.

Dinosaurs could fly.

FACT or FIB?

FEATHERED FRIENDS

Dinosaurs are related more closely to today's birds than to lizards!

FACT!

Dinosaurs like Archaeopteryx and Confuciusornis were feathered dinosaurs that could fly. Pterosaurs could fly too, but they were not dinosaurs. They were flying reptiles.

Woah!

Meat-eating dinosaurs only ate other dinosaurs.

FACT or FIB?

21

yummy!

FIB!

Some carnivorous dinosaurs ate insects, including Mononykus. For supper, it used its long claws to dig out lots of ants from tree trunks and dirt hills!

FACT or FIB?

Tyrannosaurus rex had **good breath** because it drank plenty of water.

TINY TERRORS

T. rex babies had weak legs when they first hatched. Their parents probably brought them meat to eat until they grew big enough to hunt for themselves.

Yuck!

FIB!

Tyrannosaurus rex had terrible breath! It ate meat, and some of its dinner got trapped between those giant dagger-like teeth. When the meat decayed, T. rex had terrible rot breath.

FACT or FIB?

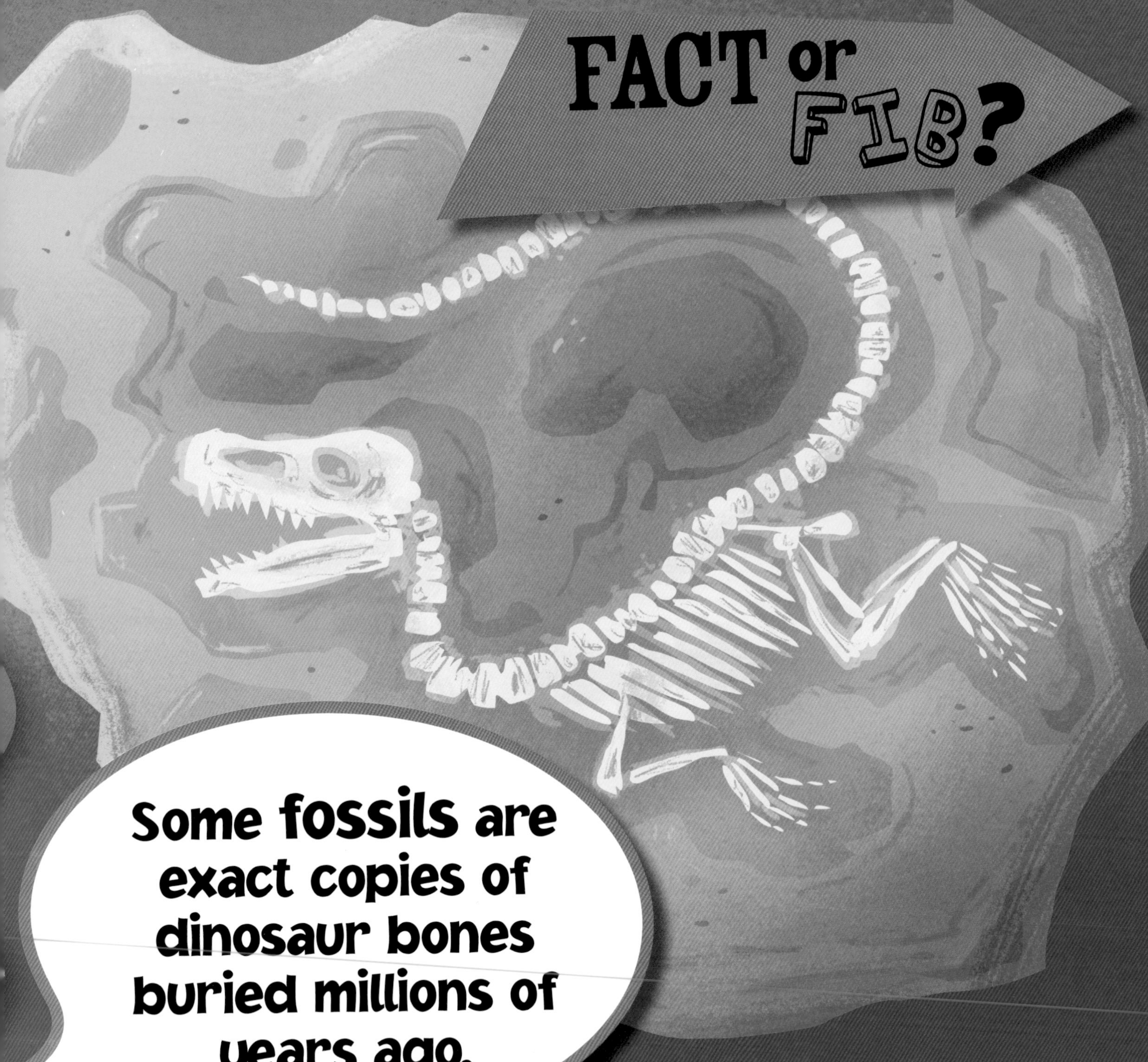

Some fossils are exact copies of dinosaur bones buried millions of years ago.

Watch out! You know what happens if you get stuck in the tar pit!

FACT!

When a dinosaur bone is gently covered in dirt, minerals in the ground water seep into tiny holes in the bone. Little by little, the minerals fill the holes and harden into rock. As the bone disappears, minerals replace it, creating an exact copy. Different minerals create different coloured fossilized bones.

FACT or FIB?

Where did everybody go?

Dinosaurs disappeared from the Earth about 66 million years ago.

FACT!

Dinosaurs did become extinct 66 million years ago. Most dinosaur scientists believe that the main reason was a giant asteroid hitting Earth. When a ten kilometre space rock slams into a planet, it really means trouble. But other things like disease and volcanic gas may have made things even worse.

Super sleuth

Asteroids can range from around the size of a pebble all the way up to 1000km across.

The end of an era...

Losing the dinosaurs to extinction may seem a little sad. But who wants to be a midnight snack to a Tyrannosaurus rex? And even the nicest long neck could still turn your house into firewood. Maybe fossilized dinosaurs are easier to love than the real thing. If not, follow the feathers! Dinosaur scientists think birds might be dinosaurs, cleverly evolved.

GUESS WHO!

No one knows for sure what dinosaurs looked like. They could have been brown, green or even pink. Scientists know that some dinos had feathers, while others had scales. Dinosaur fossils also show that some of these prehistoric creatures had special horns, spiked tails and loads of other cool body parts. Take a look at each close-up and see if you can match it to the correct dinosaur name.

3. Who owns these bone-crunching teeth?

1. Which dinosaur had feathers like these?

2. Whose horns are these?

4. Which dinosaur had spiky quills rather than scales?

CHOOSE YOUR ANSWERS FROM THE NAMES BELOW:

A. Pegomastax

B. Triceratops

C. Tyrannosaurus rex

D. Mononykus

E. Archaeopteryx

Answers: 1. E, 2. B, 3. C, 4. A, 5. D

5. Who used their long claws to eat insects?

DINO FACTS

The dinosaur with the longest name is Micropachycephalosaurus, which means 'tiny, thick-headed lizard'!

Lots of dinosaurs (like the Diplodocus) replaced their teeth – just like sharks do today! When a tooth wore out, a new one was waiting below to replace it.

The word dinosaur comes from the Greek language, and means 'terrible lizard'!

Scientists think that the fastest dinosaur was Coelophysis – and that it could run at up to 50 kilometres per hour. The fastest human speed was recorded by Usain Bolt at 44.72 kilometres per hour. Who do you think would win in a race?

Stegosaurus had the smallest brain of all the dinosaurs – it was the size of a ping-pong ball!

Scientists study fossilized dino poo to find out what they ate – yuck!

USEFUL WORDS

Asteroid – a rock (large or small) that travels round the Sun.

Carnivore – an animal that eats other animals.

Evolve – to change very slowly over a long time.

Extinction – when a species dies out.

Fossil – part of a plant or animal that has turned to stone or that has left a print of its shape in a rock.

Mineral – a natural substance found in the ground. Most rocks are made up of more than one mineral.

Prehistoric – something that existed before humans began to record history.

Pterosaur – a flying reptile that lived at the same time as the dinosaurs.

Species – a group of living things. Two animals of the same species can have babies together.